IT'S ONLY
A SHADOW

CONSTANCE MIMS

Prelude

———〜———

*"The LORD is my shepherd, I shall not want. He restores
my soul. He guides me in paths of righteousness for his
name's sake. Even though I walk through the valley of the
shadow of death, I will fear no evil, for you are with me;
your rod and your staff, they comfort me."*

Psalms 23:1, 3-4 (paraphrased)

This book bears witness to how the Lord has guided me and been with me throughout my years. Just taking comfort in knowing that God is there has been a blessing and helps me keep my sanity. Through sickness, loved ones leaving and church hurt God's promises in his word remains the same. It has taken time for me to know that when I walk with Him and followed His guidance there is victory in any situation. Some lessons I had to learn over and over and over again before I really got the understanding of what God was trying to teach me. I practiced insanity for about four years straight. I had a deja vu moment, and I finally realized that I've been here before, and it wasn't a good place. It was the same dark, cold shadow that had been lingering over me. I thank the Lord for these tests and trials that have given me this testimony to share with you. I had to learn by faith to walk in God's light. When Satan appears (and he will) to block my blessings, he steps between me and God and casts shadows of doubt, gloom, and despair upon me. In the midst of those days, I had to remember a shadow has never hurt anybody and Satan can't touch me while I'm living in God's grace. I must always check my position and keep Satan behind me. God's grace is sufficient for any situation. Remember God is no respecter of persons. What He has done for me, just ask in Jesus' name and in His will and He shall surely do the same for you. We are all at different stages in our lives. The same is true of our Christian walk. How we perform in life's trials forms the patterns in our destinies according to our faith. Just as a baby grows and becomes more confident as they get older, the more we experience the mercies of God, and the more we become confident that we can depend on God to fulfill His promises.

I write this after having tested God and finding Him to be faithful in my many times of need. It is my prayer that by relaying to you the truthful experiences of my life, your faith may also be increased.

Table of Contents

Chapter One

Just as we feed our bodies our faith must be exercised in order to develop. As a young child, you learn if you stick your hand in the fire you will get burned. Likewise, it doesn't take a rocket scientist to know if you stand in the rain, you will get wet. These are things to which no one can convince you otherwise. Because you have experienced them for yourself in one way or another, it doesn't matter how you acquired the knowledge; what matters is that you know by your own experience what will result when you are exposed to water or fire. No one can tell you anything different. Now it may have taken you more than once to reach that conclusion but once the realization is cemented in your brain, you know, that you know, that you know that fire burns and water gets you wet every time. The same is true of faith. Faith starts with a belief. You cannot have faith if you do not believe. A belief is a state of mind, it is a condition of being. It is the acceptance of material that is filtered into the brain. But to experience FAITH it must be put into action. Faith brings about an action, expectation or a move based upon a belief. "Faith without works is dead." (James 2:26)

When you have faith in something, that faith will determine your actions. Faith is developed in many different ways. For some the mere conversation from others who have gone through an experience is enough, while others may have to bump their heads in the same situation 10 times before they learn to break the cycle. Again, it is not the speed in which you learn the lesson, but it is the assurance that you gain in the fact that you can trust God to fulfill your needs. One thing is for sure, there cannot be an increase in spiritual growth without an increase in one's faith. They go hand in hand.

Chapter Two

I was raised in a family with religious values. Although my family structure in my early youth was not the traditional home composed of the mother dad and kids, there was plenty of love within my clan like family. Attending church was a must even if the adults did not go each Sunday. Reverend John Hoover was the Pastor of an established Baptist church. He was a stout, dark complexioned man, whose voice boomed when he spoke. Yet he had a gentle spirit when he spoke to the children. He always took time to talk and answer our questions. Even back then I was quick to ask about things I did not understand.

I remember asking him once about the voice that I would hear during the sermons. I told him that sometimes I would hear a voice that would tell me to get up and join the church while another would tell me to stay seated. Until then I had listened to the latter. Reverend Hoover explained to me that it was God speaking to me asking me to come give my heart to him and the devil trying to prevent me from doing so. There was no fire and brimstone explanation, just simply for me to listen to the voice that was strongest. I accepted the Lord Jesus as my Savior on a Thursday night during a revival at the age of seven. Although Pastor Hoover was only in my life for less than 12 years, his teaching had a great influence on the development of my character and moral values. Under his guidance I learned how to pray.

I put the power of prayer to the test for the first time when I was in the 5th grade. I had a teacher that I truly did not like when I was in the 1st grade and when I reached grade five, I had the misfortune to have her as my teacher once again. She was the kind of teacher that played up to the parents when they came to the school but was mean as the devil when they weren't there. Of course, my mother loved her. Mom would visit the school often and I always hoped she would catch her the way we saw her, but she never did. I was a good student and received excellent grades however at the end of one grading period, the teacher told me that I was going to receive a bad grade. In my household that was a no-no. I feared I was going to get the whipping of my life. So, for about a week before the grades were read, I prayed with all my heart that God would have mercy and not let me get anything less than a C. Although a C was going to place me on punishment, anything less in my mind would have been close to a death sentence. As she went down the row calling out grades when she got to my name, she stopped to tell me once again, "I told you that you were going to get a bad grade. You have a C." I had to fight back the smile that I was feeling down deep within. All that kept running through my mind was pray works, it works, prayer works. That was my first real experience with God. I now know that faith is the substance of things hoped for and the evidence of things not seen. However, at that time I did not know enough about scripture to trust and believe. I only knew I had to call out for help from someone and I couldn't tell anyone else. So, God was it. How much easier life would be if we would handle all our problems that way. As we get older we feel we can handle it ourselves, and only after we make the situation much worse do we give it over to God.

Chapter Three

I grew up the product of a single mother who was raised by a village. I was born in Trenton, Kentucky. My mother had me at an early age, so I was basically raised by my grandmother and the family. When I was just three weeks old our house caught on fire. Mom, being so young and new to motherhood, ran out of the house and forgot me in the burning building. My Aunt Rosetta had to tell her to go back to get me. That was the start of my life and a pattern for what seemed to occur for the years to come. I felt the need to constantly remind people that I did exist. I even had to remind myself at times that there was a purpose for my life.

"Big Mama" as we called her, played a special part in my life. My life was filled with love, and I was pampered to the point of being spoiled. Not like a nasty brat, but I was spoiled. She would do everything and anything to make me happy. She actually dressed me until I was in the second grade. She was only 4ft' 11 inches tall with a little waist but a huge bottom and her heart was even bigger.

Johnetta Coleman had the sweetest, kindest heart of anyone you could imagine. There was always room in the house and a place at the table to eat for anyone in need. She was a true believer. She would talk about the Lord and pray. Her Christianity showed in her actions. However, she rarely went to church. But she made sure that me and my cousin Rosemary attended Sunday School, Bible study and choir practice every week. She stayed home to cook dinner. Sunday dinner's menu was always the same, fried chicken, mashed potatoes, peas and cornbread. Sometimes we would have greens instead of peas, but the meat was almost always chicken. If we were lucky, we would get a nickel pack of red Kool-Aid. I can almost smell and taste her chicken just thinking about it.

In the early school years, I was my mother's only child. Big Mama and Mom both worked for white families as housekeepers. Big Mama worked for the Fitzgerald family until she retired. They had a large family of nine children. Their only daughter was my age and was named Mary Jane. Sometimes in the summer I would go to work with her. Mary Jane taught me how to climb the tree in her backyard with a high fence. When we were climbing high in the tree, we were both hidden from the world, and that fence blocked out all the racism that surrounded us. This was a few years before Dr. Martin Luther King delivered his famous "I Had a Dream" speech.

Chapter Four

We were poor but I didn't know it. My family moved to Evansville, Indiana right after the fire. We literally created a family village. Everyone lived in a two-block radius of each other. Aunt Rosetta was one block to the north, Uncle Bubba and Annabelle lived around the corner on the next street and Aunt Jessie and Uncle Jim lived just two blocks across the street to the east of our home. My mother Mary, Uncle Robert and Big Mama lived in the same house right behind the #9 fire station. It was the nucleus of the family structure.

My cousin Rosemary and I were the only children at the time. Aunt Rosetta had been married and separated from her husband Junior and was always on the go doing her own thing. She would leave Rosemary with my mom and Big Mama the majority of the time but was there when needed. Even with that and the foundation of my immediate family, I felt Rosa had it a little better than I. She knew her daddy and all I had was a name. My uncles used to tease me by saying the buzzards had me and the sun hatched me. It hurt me but they never knew. I had my uncles and that seemed to be enough at that time. It's funny how you seem to have a favorite relative. Uncle Robert was always the smart one in school, played sports and hung out with the popular fine-looking guys. They even had a little singing doo-wop group (of course) Rosemary and I had a secret crush on the two of them. They played along with us, and we took it to heart. Then Uncle Robert had his birthday party and the real girlfriends showed up. We were crushed. Robert was Rosemary's favorite.

Uncle Bubba was loud, cussed almost every other word and drank a lot. He had an older girlfriend named Annabelle who took care of him regardless of how he behaved. She thought that he could do no wrong and neither did I. I loved me some Uncle Bubba. He would cuss me (in a loving affectionate way of course) but dragged Rosemary and I behind him giving us everything that he could afford. One of my fondest memories is when I got a hula hoop. I loved to do it. We didn't have a car so when it was time for me to go to kindergarten the next day, I wanted to take it with me. Of course, Mom said no, and I started to cry. Uncle Bubba grabbed the hula hoop from my mom and took it out of the house. He walked beside me the whole eight blocks or more to school while I hula hooped. At the end of the day, he met me with it so I could hula hoop all the way back. That was my Uncle Bubba.

Rosemary and I never really got into any trouble. We did silly things of course. I remember we liked the taste of Alka-Seltzer and let them fizzle in our mouths. Mom bought a large bottle. She usually would not notice but this time I guess we took too many. When she asked what happened to them, we both said, "I don't know." She kept pressuring us to tell the truth. Big Mama said, "Leave them girls alone. They didn't get in those things, and you probably took them and don't remember it."

It was around Christmas time. Mom announced, "I know what I'm going to do. I'm going to call Santa at Sears and have him talk to you." But we had our stories and we were sticking to it. Then the phone rings. My mother answers and says, "Thanks Santa for calling me back." When she held the phone out to Rosemary and says, "Santa wants to talk to you," my cousin hit the floor while crying and screaming. I stood there in shock. Mom put the phone in my hand and I heard a deep voice that asked, "Connie have you been naughty?" I quickly said yes and volunteered that we took turns going into the bathroom and ate the Alka Seltzers. Big Mama was speechless. Uncle Robert and Mom were laughing so hard they didn't give us a whooping I guess we had whipped ourselves. I didn't find out until I was in my 40's that Santa Claus was Uncle Robert's best friend Walter Brown. Life for me at 6 years of age took a whole new spin. I was told for the first time I actually had a father. He wanted me to come to visit him in New York. Mom dressed me up and sent me on a plane by myself. I remember the plane ride vividly. I was greeted by this tall handsome man that introduced himself as my father. I found out I had a little sister named Sharon who was only four years old at the time. I only saw her maybe two or three times the whole time that I was there. But I spent most of my summer with Aunt Mary and my cousins, Robin and Ricky. On occasion I would go to my Nana's home. Dad usually picked me up on the weekends because of his work schedule.

Robin was very pretty with the Becky-with-the-good-hair look. She was a little bit on the chubby side but a very happy and loving kid. She had a wonderful smile and a beautiful attitude. We had lots of fun that summer. Ricky was a little older and didn't spend much time with us other than to joke around and swim in their pool. At the end of the summer my mother came to pick me up. After returning to Evansville, Indiana two weeks later my mother returned back to New York without me. She stayed there for about a year, and I stayed at home with Big Mama. I guess she went to see if they could work it out. But just as quickly and suddenly as my father had come into my life he was gone and did not appear again until I was 22 and had a child of my own. I was told in addition to Sharon I had another sister named Sabrina. After years of little communication, I developed a relationship with my biological father and my extended family members.

Chapter Five

Although Mom dropped out of school in the 10th grade, I was told repeatedly how smart she had been in school. She worked hard but never missed the opportunity to volunteer at school and attend parent teacher meetings. I didn't get a chance to get in trouble because every time I turned around, she was at the school or helping with an activity. As a result, all the teachers knew me. I was overly protected by my uncles and my mother was very strict. I appreciate it now but back then it wasn't easy. Without a formal education my mother took on cleaning jobs to handle the financial responsibilities of me, her mother and her youngest brother. She was a strong hard-working woman with a desire to have better things in life. Although pregnant at an early age she wasn't what you'd call a "street" woman. She never really drank, cussed or hung out in the clubs. Her life consisted mainly of being at work and taking care of her family. When I was about to enter the seventh grade in the late 60's, it was around the time of desegregation of the schools, and my mother made sure that I was one of the only 13 students in Vanderburgh County to attend one of the

White schools in the system. That summer everyone teased me and told me: "Those White folks are going to have you hanging from a tree." I was scared to death by the time I got to the first day of school. But I found out that desegregation actually made me more popular! I was one of only three Blacks that went to middle school which made me stand out. So, by the second day everybody knew my name. Just about everyone was nice and they treated me well. There were a few that used the n-word and made nasty comments, but for the most part it was a great experience for me as well as some of the other children who had never seen a Black person before. Mama made the best out of her life.

She got married when I was in the 6th grade and moved to Marion, Indiana. I remained at home with Big Mama. My absentee father was replaced by Mr. Clayton Ware. I did not really care for him when i first met him. After a few years I would come to realize he was exactly what was missing in my life.

In the middle of my 8th grade year of school, I went to live with my mother and stepfather. (Just saying the words stepfather now seems unnatural. He became my father in every sense of the word). He was an excellent father. I can't say stepfather because he never treated me as if I was a step anything. He provided the money for every school affair and

23

was always there to encourage. I learned first-hand from him what a man should do and how he is to take care of his family.

Mom never wanted for anything that he had the ability to provide. At first, I was timid, and I would ask Mom for things I needed. It didn't take long for me to realize she would go to him for what I needed. So, I started just bypassing her altogether and learned when I needed something to go to Clayton and ask for it myself. If it was a need the answer was always yes. Clayton had two boys a little younger than me, but I was the only child living in our household until I became 18 years old. My mother then gave birth to two sons, Avis and Toby. My dad always made it known that I was the princess of the house. He showed himself to be a great provider and a man of character. He was a man of his word. If Clayton Ware said it, you could take it to the bank. Because of his love and encouragement, I learned that I was precious and worthy of respect. Because of him I was not a pushover for the lines of boys. I know God sent him to rescue me and my mom. When Avis was born, I was a proud big sister. He was such a happy outgoing baby. I carried him around everywhere. Everybody thought he was my baby, and they swore that my mom was just saying Avis was hers just to protect my reputation. Only 13 months later my youngest brother Toby was born. He was the complete opposite and only a Mama's baby. Unfortunately, soon after he was born, I was off for the first time away from home to attend Tennessee State University.

Chapter Six

My high school years were pretty good experiences for me. I had been reasonably popular in school and didn't have any problems. I was active in several activities and clubs and received a few awards. So, I thought I was pretty much prepared for college life. Nothing could have been further from the truth.

Over the years although my love for Uncle Bubba did not change, my role model became Uncle Robert. He attended Pinewood Jr. College and then Alcorn College in Mississippi to complete his bachelor's degree. Uncle Robert was the first person in our family to attend college. I really looked up to him and I wanted to follow in his footsteps. I heard about the sororities and fraternities and how great it was to have freedom to make your own choices. I looked forward to campus life. I really thought I was ready for it.

After attending predominantly white schools I developed a false sense that all of the world had gotten over racial prejudice simply because it had not seriously affected me. Lord, thank you for my blinders at that time. It allowed me to be open to the fact that harmony between the races can exist. This belief is what would prove to separate me from many of my black peers at the College. Their views and mine often clashed. My life experiences were quite different from their reality. They thought I was living in a fantasy world, and I couldn't embrace the anger and distrust that they possessed.

Going to a predominantly Black Southern College proved to be a more difficult adjustment than the first year that I participated in the desegregation in middle school. I experienced culture shock to the umpteenth degree. It was like stepping into another dimension. My normality did not exist in that part of that world. My expectation for a campus of unity and camaraderie was not to be found. From the first time I opened my mouth I was judged for not speaking like a Black person. The Southern culture that I was being exposed to and the way I had been raised called for an adjustment that I was not prepared to make. There were so many different prejudices. Dark-skinned people didn't like the uppity high yellow ones, Northern against Southern, fat against skinny. There were so many other prejudices that they overshadowed the Black/White issues for which the South was known.

For the first time in a long time, I felt as though I didn't fit in. I thought I had overcome those fears, but it was like being pushed into a corner again it seemed nothing I said was right. The way I dressed wasn't like what southern girls wore. Everything was upside-down.

But I did find my niche. My mother's second hustle was doing hair. She was self-taught and very good at it. The state cosmetology board called on her several times because she was taking many clients from the professional shops. So, I learned how to do hair by watching her. When I got to college, I often made extra money doing hair. I would do a press and curl for $1.50 and a simple press for $1. That was a lot of money for the girls in the dorm because we didn't have a good two nickels after tuition. It kept a little extra change in my pocket.

I soon found out that all of my grandmother's pampering and doing everything for me actually turned out to be a hindrance. My first set of clothes that I had to wash all turned pink. I had no idea whatsoever how to wash clothes or take care of anything. All I knew was how to keep my hair going and that was it. As a result, I struggled while there and wasted Mom's hard-earned money. During the time that I was there I partied and slept most of the time. I didn't start paying attention to my classes until close to the end of the year. Unfortunately, my time at Tennessee State University was cut short as a result of being raped. My mother and Uncle Robert came to pick me up. The experience was so traumatic that I withdrew and returned home. I felt defeated. I left with the thought that I would return to finish my studies the next year. But my life's road map had many detours. It turned out to be 15 years before I earned my first degree.

Chapter Seven

After returning home, I got a job at a local nursing home. I no longer wanted to return to the summer job I had worked for three years as a lifeguard. It was time now for me to move on to my big girl world and make more money. I spent most of my time taking care of my two younger brothers because mom worked nights. That wasn't a problem, but I soon felt the urge to want more and the need to get out on my own. I couldn't wait to be my own boss.

Chapter Eight

I moved to Indianapolis with my best friend Debbie. We had been friend's ever since middle school. She moved into an apartment a year before I joined her in Indianapolis. During that time, we really didn't go out to party much, and she acquired her own set of friends. I started thinking that I really didn't feel comfortable not going to a church or being affiliated with any spiritual connection.

The principles that were set by Aunt Jesse and Uncle Jim and what they taught me stuck in my mind. They seemed to be what you would call a perfect Christian family. One of them would come pick up Rosemary and I to take us to children's choir practice every week. Whenever I visited with them, we would have Bible study inside their home. They would pray and read the Bible to us. It made me feel like that was the real Christian life. This was something I wanted to imitate in my adult life. It seemed not to be just talk where they would do something on Sunday and then in the middle of the week it is something different. That wasn't what was going on in my own home. There wasn't that strong sense of a daily Christian walk. However, for reasons I didn't understand, and I can't explain, Uncle Jim and Aunt Jessie end up getting a divorce. I was told it was because of Uncle Jim's infidelity with a neighbor. I couldn't wrap my head around how people that appear to be walking according to God would end up separating?

It took a while for me to realize we're all only human with imperfections. Shortly after joining the church in Indianapolis a friend that I was dating off and on for a couple of years from Evansville got in contact with me. He was my Big Mama's paper boy. I told my mother while walking up the street to my aunt's house, "That's the guy I like and I'm going to marry him." I guess I was only 12 or 13 years old then. Mama laughed and said, "Well, he's already got a job." His name was Arthur Levester but his family in Evansville called him Tommy. At the time, Tommy was attending a Bible study group on Saturday evenings at his co-worker's home, William Smith, who was also his best friend. He asked me to come along. It wasn't long after that we started getting closer and closer and after about a year, we were married and very active in church.

William and Denise became our best friends. Denise and I had several of our kids around the same time. We mainly attended church and took care of families. They became my children's godparents, and we were theirs.

Somehow things started changing. The rules and regulations of the church started getting stricter on women. Scriptures were being used about how a woman was supposed to submit to her husband and women started not wearing makeup and wearing long dresses. I was beginning to get that closed-in feeling again like I was being held down like I was under water. The men in the group were good men with really good intentions but they had taken "women into submission" out of context and they were beginning to use it as a means of control. All the men were the breadwinners and the wives had to stay home, take care of the kids, and cook dinner.

I remember Denise and I would go out someplace during the day and we'd have to make a special effort to keep track of time so we could get home in time to prepare dinner and be there before our husbands walked in the door. I began to take the teachings that we were being taught to heart. I started baking homemade bread every day in addition to making sure my husband had a full-course meal with no leftovers when he came home from work.

But there was something missing in my life after the birth of my first daughter, Aletha. For one thing, I started to gain weight because many of my days were spent sitting at the house doing nothing. I was unhappy and although I loved cooking every day, I was feeling miserable about myself.

When Aletha turned four years old, I decided I wanted to become a cosmetologist even though I hadn't gone to school for it.

The good thing was that I was already doing hair at home. When I asked my husband how he felt about me going to beauty school he told me no. He said the woman's place was supposed to be in the house, and he wasn't going to pay for it.

Despite his objection, I applied to Michael's Beauty College anyway. In order to get a grant, I lied and told the staff I was separated from my husband. I spoke with one of my dear friends at the church and asked her to babysit my daughter, but when I returned that afternoon after my first day of school, she told me that she could no longer keep my daughter because I was out of the will of God by being disobedient to my husband. I said okay and thanked her. The next day I enrolled Aletha in the private Christian School where some of our church members had their children enrolled. Tommy could not complain because she was school age. I limited my hours for class to fit her school schedule. This was the beginning embarquement of a total change that would affect me for the rest of my life.

Chapter Nine

I entered beauty school with a head full of natural, unprocessed hair which was not popular at that time. It didn't take long for me to realize that everyone in class was very conscious of fashion, hair styles and makeup and had been exposed to a world that I had no idea existed. For most of my life I have been sheltered and never experienced any drugs or the fast life.

After several weeks I was talked into relaxing my hair, arching my eyebrows and starting to wear makeup by my classmates at the school.

This was not acceptable to my husband or the other members of the church, and I began feeling like an outcast again. Why was I being more accepted by those considered "worldly people" than my own church? These were people that were supposed to be non-judgmental. Why weren't they showing me the Christian love that they talked about every day? Some of the women in the church supported me by allowing me to do their hair but they would not defend me to their husbands. I started to help them with little changes to their makeup. The men of the church told my husband he needed to get his wife in check. I was devastated. I was learning new skills and I recognized that I was really good at my new career. But as happy as that made me, I was getting even more distraught and unhappy with being under the control and judgmental stares from my church members and unkind remarks.

In one incident I was asked to attend a party by one of my fellow classmates who was gay. We were good friends at school, and it was his birthday. I knew Tommy would not be kind to him so I didn't ask him to go with me nor did I discuss if I should attend. When I arrived, he actually had a very nice penthouse apartment in Indianapolis. The place was full of people. While walking into the entryway, I saw someone with long flowing hair sitting in the lap of a man. When they turned around it was obvious that it was two men kissing. I had never experienced that before. I must say I was still fascinated by what was going on. Something was telling me I needed to get out and run, but I was curious and wanted to stay because everybody was friendly. They were talking to me and complimenting my hair and makeup. This wasn't a judgmental atmosphere not anywhere in the room.

When I got home, I explained what happened and what I'd seen. Of course, the description of the party made him even more determined that I had absolutely no business attending the school and if I continued to go, I definitely would not be ALLOWED to attend another party.

I had gotten a pretty good clientele at the school and developed some new friends. I found myself torn between my new friends whispering in my ear that my husband was too controlling, and on the other hand my Christian friends. My old friends were being judgmental of my new clothes and the way that I liked being able to make money of my own. It felt good that I didn't have to succumb to my husband's every wish to keep my own money in my pocket.

I started a journey to better myself physically and mentally. When I was in school, I was always known to have a pretty mom. Everybody would say your mom is so pretty and I wanted to have the same thing for my daughter Aletha. When I looked at myself and the shape of my body, I didn't like the way that I looked. I knew that I wasn't putting my best foot forward for my child and I didn't want that, so I decided to have the bariatric bypass surgery to help me lose the weight.

During the consultation with the bariatric doctor, he explained to my husband all the different things that could go wrong and that he would not perform the operation without both our signatures. Tommy said, "No, we're not doing it." I told the doctor if he did not sign the papers then I would get a divorce and come back and have it done. Reluctantly, he agreed to sign the papers. Dr. John Huses said at that time the divorce rate for people to get the bariatric surgery is very high. He asked us, "Are you sure you guys want to do this? If you do, I suggest you go to counseling."

I didn't realize how true those words would be. After about a year I lost 150 pounds, then I became pregnant with my second child, Adrian.

I wanted to get my tubes tied after the birth, but my mother and my husband talked me out of it. I found myself pregnant again four months later. My daughters, Adrian and Angela are only 10 months apart. Even with me having children Tommy became more and more jealous. He started questioning where I went and how long I was going to be gone. The more he questioned me and tried to control me the more rebellious I became. One night after years of not seeing each other my girlfriend Debbie and I reconnected, and we went out for girls night out. It was totally innocent. We went downtown to watch a band that was playing. After the set ended there was an after-party in another part of the hotel for the band and the band members' friends. It ended late and I arrived home past three o'clock in the morning. Nothing happened; we were just simply catching up on things talking, laughing, dancing and drinking.

When I got home Tommy was extremely upset. I told him nothing happened and just let it go. For the first time in our relationship my normally gentle-natured husband turned physically abusive. Now he did not hit me nor beat me up, but he straddled me on the bed and held me down for what seemed like hours asking me repeatedly: "Who was it? Who was he?" There wasn't a "he" to tell him about and I felt that his temperament and jealousy was getting worse and worse so when he finally went to sleep, I gathered my kids and walked out during the middle of the night. I left my car in the driveway so I wouldn't wake him. I walked the five blocks to our friends' Denise and Williams house. The next day I called a shelter for battered women.

Chapter Ten

Until then my husband had been an excellent provider. He paid all the bills and we went on vacation every year. He was an all-around good man that loved the Lord. The fact of the matter is I simply outgrew him, and he did not want to be part of my world. His controlling ways drove a wedge between us. Neither of us considered going to counseling. I refused to listen to one-sided advice from spiritual leaders.

Chapter Eleven

I found a job as a Cosmetology Instructor and I was making decent money. I even had a new car that I purchased myself. I returned to get my car the following day and proceeded to the shelter. I had everything planned. I had a good paying job, and I would be getting paid the following week. I figured it would only take a couple of weeks for me to find an apartment of my own and get re-established on my own. Mom and Clayton came to the shelter. They begged me to come home with them.

Since Aletha was almost ten years old and I was concerned about which school she would have to attend, I agreed to let my mother take her back to her home in Marion, Indiana which was 65 miles away and the two younger ones were only 2 and 3 and stayed at the shelter with me. Three days later my mother called to inform me that she enrolled Aletha in Avis and Toby's private school because there would not be an additional charge for a third child.

What could I say, I didn't have anything better to offer and I just knew it would only be a matter of a couple weeks before I would get her back. However, I didn't realize that when you enter a shelter you have to apply for food stamps. When I gave the intake person the information and I filled out the forms, the first thing she said was even I don't have a late model car like this. She told me I had to take a copy of the forms to my employer to verify my income for the food stamps. When I gave the form to the school owner, his reply was, "Well if you're at a shelter I don't know if we want to have our employees working for us and they are practically homeless. When you get your life together then you can come back, and you can have a job." Just like that, I lost my job.

Two days later when I got up to go looking for another job, I realized my car was gone. When the shelter called the police department, we found out that my car was repossessed. I called the car lot and was informed the shelter called them and told them I was at the shelter for battered women. The car dealership assumed I would not have the ability to pay for the car, so they repossessed it. I went from having a stable home with a decent job and a car with a husband taking care of all the household bills to not having transportation or a job. To make matters worse, my two youngest children had severe asthma and could not eat half of the food that they prepared in the shelter. The food stamps that I signed for were given to the facility and did not benefit me and my children at all. The decision to allow my mother to take my daughter home with her; even though it was in an attempt to help me, turned out to be a fatal mistake. Aletha remained in the Marion school system and in her grandparent's control for two years. Unfortunately, it drove a wedge between myself and my daughter. She resents our time apart and often mentions why I chose to keep the other two children while sending her away. What was supposed to be a two-week stay turned into five months.

My divorce was finalized three days before Christmas while I was still a resident of the shelter.

Chapter Twelve

Truth be told, I went from my mother's house where I had to go by her rules and regulations to an even more controlled environment with my husband. Even though things were not the best living at the shelter, I was free! There wasn't anyone to tell me what to do or where to go. I was making up my own rules on my own terms. I was in control of my life now and I was determined to live it to the fullest. Lord, I thank you for your grace and mercy for keeping me.

Somewhere in the madness I decided I wanted to get my bachelor's degree. I enrolled in another Black college, Martin Center University, in Indianapolis and completed my bachelor's degree. My education and business career were on an upswing but for some reason my personal life continued to spiral downward and out of control. I had a quick rebound marriage after my divorce from the kid's father in which I learned the real definition of physical abuse.

The first time I experienced his anger was when he came home for lunch. I was feeding my daughters, Adrian and Angela, who were three and four years old at the time. He saw that I gave them the leftovers from the night before (which evidently he had his mind set on for himself). He made the comment, "In his father's house men got to eat first and the kids got what was left over." This immediately gave me a flashback of the controlling spirit that I was under before. When I responded, "No, I'm not feeding anyone before I feed my children." He told me to shut the "F" up. Me not ever having to be scared before yelled back at him with the same rage: "NO YOU SHUT THE F... UP!" He hit me with his fist full force in my eye. I started screaming then the girls began crying so loud the old lady next door made him open the door. My eye immediately closed. He had given me a huge, swollen black eye that was so bad I had to go to the hospital that night. All the way there he kept saying he was sorry, and it would never happen again. He even managed to shed tears.

The staff at the hospital asked if I was safe. I didn't want to repeat the situation of being in the shelter again, so I lied and remained in the relationship.

Along with the physical and mental abuse came infidelity. The final straw was when he took my car and stayed out all night. By the time he got home the next morning the kids were getting on the bus to go to school.

When I asked him where he had been he didn't answer. He laid the keys on the counter, and I reached for them. He tried to get the keys first, but I beat him to them. That angered him and he began beating me. He punched me several times in the face or wherever he could land a blow. Finally, he knocked me to the floor and started kicking me. He abruptly stopped and stood over me and said, "I'm going to kill you." Since he had a history of mental issues, he told me on several occasions that he could kill me and never do a day of jail time. He headed toward the bedroom where I knew we had a gun underneath the mattress. I jumped up and ran toward the front door. I grabbed a coat from the closet because I still had on my night clothes.

I bolted outside and got into the car and locked the doors. Somehow the keys had gotten tangled in my hair. All of a sudden, he came running out of the house and jumped on the hood of the car. He looked at me through the windshield and yelled, "I'm going to kill you!" I put the car in reverse and sped out of the driveway. I drove past my children's school bus and onto the main road for about a couple miles until I came to a railroad crossing. A train was coming but I knew if I stopped, he was going to bust the window and hurt me.

I made a U-turn in the center of the street and came back by the school on the corner. Students were going into the building and parents were dropping their kids off. By this time cars were following us blowing their horns. Several male construction workers in their work trucks had joined in the chase to help. The whole time he was continuing to yell he was going to kill me. Finally, I drove upon the curve of the school yard and slammed on brakes. I don't know how fast I was driving but he was thrown off the car.

I jumped out of the car bloody, bruised and with my hair and face a mess. I screamed for help and was quickly surrounded by the people who had been following me. He started limping while bent down holding his shoulder trying to walk away. The police arrived within seconds as several people had called for help. I found out later that he had broken his clavicle bone and several ribs from being thrown off the car.

When I was able to leave the scene, I immediately went to my attorney's office, and had him draw papers for the divorce. My husband was served when he attended his court hearing. The sheriff handed him the papers and told him to just sign it and that was the end of that dramatic relationship. At that point I realized my problems with my first husband was not so bad. My impatience for him to adjust to the changes in our relationship and making a rash decision to run away had placed me in a much darker and dangerous position. The girls were able to spend time with him every other weekend, and my mother or his mother wanted them on school vacations. After the first couple of years Tommy and I learned how to co-parent. We (and both sides of their family) made sure they were well.

Except for the period when I was at Tennessee State I was sheltered by my parents and then by my husband of 11 years. That was most of my life. For a good four years I found my natural (worldly) mind. I didn't look toward a church. Some people like to say "I thought I was having fun back then" when they speak about their youth and how they behaved and honestly for that time and that season I did have fun in that moment. I started doing everything that I was told I couldn't do. I broke of all the rules except drugs. I was too scared to try something that I couldn't control. Not even weed. Nothing in me wanted to be loyal to a husband at that moment. I felt a betrayal of the church's overly judgmental ways. I devoted half my life going to Bible study and religious services to end up hurt and abused mentally and physically by people who claimed to love me. I had no desire, nor did I want to associate with religious people anymore. I was tired of trying to fit in. I felt like a failure around churchy folks, so I went to the side that welcomed me. The dark side.

I started going out to clubs almost every night. I made new friends that encouraged me to show off my new body. We never paid to go into the club. Somebody always knew someone at the door, or we got to know them. I worked hard and partied harder. But deep in my heart I still wanted and missed a spiritual life. I desired the long-term relationship like my mother had with Clayton. But it was elusive, and I was impatient and pretended not to care. So, I settled for casual relationships that ended in someone having a broken heart. Sometimes it was mine that was torn to pieces. I had my share of gentlemen that were different races, some rich and some poor. I indulged myself in living the single life.

I had a few boy toys that I played with and some of the boys played with me. On my 40th birthday one of my younger friends named Lisa threw me a party at a local club. Without my knowledge she ordered a stripper for me. Just before he came out, she could not keep the secret and told me what the surprise was. She said his stage name was Midnight. She went on to say how fine and wonderfully built the stripper was because she knew I was picky. When

Midnight came to the stage, I was surprised to see he was someone I had been dating regularly.

I knew I had come to the end of the line. There was nothing left to do. I was tired of seeing and doing the same thing just to fill time and space. There had to be a purpose for my life. I decided it was time to get myself and my girls back into fellowship with God. I had to find a Bible-teaching church that was under good leadership.

Chapter Thirteen

―――――∽―――――

Proverbs 22:6 (NIV)

"Train up a child in the way he should go, and when he is old he will not depart from it".

I have heard that scripture a million times, but I know first-hand that I'm a product of it. My spirit took me back to the days of being at my Aunt Jessie and Uncle Jim's house when they would read the Bible and pray with Rosemary and I when we stayed the weekend with them. I missed the weekend Bible studies with Tommy and our circle of friends. I longed to return back to those things but not particularly under the same circumstances. I longed for the spiritual connection I had before with God. I wanted to seek His face once again.

I found myself in a place where I had to look at what I was doing and how different I was living my life from the way I was brought up. Although my mother had gotten pregnant with me at age 14, she made sure that I was under someone to give me spiritual guidance.

Now, here I was much older and having been married and taught the word of God giving my children much less than she did. A shame passed over me that I never felt before. God had exposed me in every way. At only nine years old I was being exposed to the teaching of the Bible. Rev. Hoover always stressed in Bible study that I was to always read the scripture for myself and not to accept anything that someone told me if they cannot provide proof of it in the written Word. Somehow, I lost track of those precious words of wisdom.

In afterthought I realized that a lot of the things that I was taught in my young adult life was misquoted or taken out of context. My heart wanted to be in agreement with my religious friends because we developed a bond based on what I believed to be the Word of God. But with my lack of knowledge, I was led to believe when I rejected their controlling ways, I was rejecting God. I came to the revelation that I had to find a place where my children and I could learn under good sound doctrine.

We started attending a local church. My girls were in middle school, and my house was the neighborhood house where all the kids came after school, primarily because I did not trust them going into somebody else's home. When my kids were home with me, I knew what they were doing and where they were.

I decided to start a Bible study program with the kids. I know most of them came for fun and entertainment afterward. But they got a little bit of the word. I only taught what I knew, which was the life of Jesus and the plan of salvation.

The kids would come on Saturday and listen to half an hour of Bible study. For some this was the first time they ever held a Bible or heard anything about the word of God. The study grew to the point that I told my pastor that I was going to have the kids sleep over and bring them with me to church. Someone called the media and the TV station showed up at the Bible study and interviewed them. I was not prepared for the 74 for kids that showed up that night. But no one was turned away. I had a small three-bedroom house, and they slept wherever they could find a place.

The next Sunday morning we walked the seven blocks to the church. I will never forget looking back and seeing the line of young people following me to the church. The pastor was surprised to see so many children who filled up the back of the church. They were given Bibles at the door. Out of the 74 children, 36 got saved that day not to mention the others who had accepted Christ in the Bible studies the weeks before.

Once again when things were going well up jumps the devil. I was still in search of my soul mate. I was attempting to get my life on the right track and was cleaning up my bad habits. The clean up called for a restructuring of my life. I was in a dysfunctional relationship with a man who had a wonderful personality and could be very caring. The problem was he was an alcoholic. His alcoholism prevented him from being a provider and he would become extremely jealous while intoxicated. He wasn't saved but I thought I could be a good influence on him, and we would live happily ever after. I compounded the situation by marrying him because of the religious pressure I was receiving. Instead of waiting for God to send me a man and staying abstinent I chose to marry rather than to burn. Lord, how ignorant I was at that time. I took the easy way out instead of waiting and leaning on the Lord.

We have all heard how preachers compare our ability to understand and devour the Word of God like food. Babies drink milk, toddlers eat pablum and teens soft foods and finally the mature are able to consume and digest meat. A good preacher delivers meat that can be understood by all, or it will be regurgitated and have no nutritional value. I was suffering from spiritual bulimia. I was hearing the Word, but it was being distorted or misquoted so what I thought I knew in reality I really didn't have a true understanding of what God had for me. Then tragedy happened. One morning as the children were getting ready for school, an electrical fire broke out in my two-story home. Adrian was downstairs (thank God, because of her fear of heights and weight problem she would not have gotten out of the upstairs windows.) Aletha, Angela and I were trapped upstairs.

The fire spread from the closet under the stairs so quickly all I could do was to tell Adrian to go outside while the girls and I ran back to the bedrooms. The smoke was so thick that my daughters and I got separated into different bedrooms.

Adrian ran to the neighbor's house to call the fire department. We all had to jump from the second story. Aletha pushed her younger sister out of the window where she was caught. The windows were narrow and sled horizontal and were high from the floor. Aletha had a very hard time trying to jump up to get out of the window and actually received burns on both her sides from the metal frames as she was pulled out by her fingertips by my husband on a ladder. Angela saw that she was falling headfirst and dove under her, breaking her fall. I was on the front side of the house leaning out of my bedroom window. I could see the flames at the doorway behind me and felt the heat before I tried to jump out of the window. Unfortunately, my robe got caught on something which exposed my naked body to the news helicopters. When the cloth gave way, I fell to the ground causing me to break my back. I remained in a wheelchair for close to three months.

Chapter Fourteen

After the fire while in a drunken rage the man I had married was arrested and sentenced to prison. I used what was left from the insurance money and opened a salon and eventually a beauty college. I rededicated my life to Christ. Through all this I continued to be placed in a position to help, mentor and share love with numerous youths from troubled homes. I didn't call it a ministry then because I didn't feel I was worthy to be used by God.

The businesses were doing well, and I made it a point to be active in my community. I achieved numerous awards and recognition in the cosmetology and business industry. I was a regular on a weekly Christian radio program which led to me being asked to host a television show. Financially and spiritually, I was thriving. Not just thriving, I was doing very well. I was good at what I did. I developed good people skills and was talented in hair design but after paying my tithes, I spent money like water. I splurged on my girls. They called the limousine service like taxi cabs. They were good, well-mannered children so I was happy to do it for them.

It wasn't that I wasn't used to having money. My stepfather provided my every need and most of my wants, so I never lacked material things. Spending money gave me a false feeling of security. I became dependent on money instead of relying on God as I had in the past. To put it simply I was not a good steward of the money with which God had blessed me. I lived in a fairly large city, but there were only four beauty colleges from which to choose. I sponsored a lot of activities that I thought would encourage the youth.

On one occasion, the host of another TV show asked me to sponsor a talent show which was to showcase local kid's talents. When I went to one of the rehearsals a middle-aged woman got up on the stage and announced that she was a pastor and was glad to be a sponsor. I grew up in an old southern Baptist church, and along with the teaching from the cult-like beliefs that were drilled into my head from my first marriage, the words she spoke caused the hairs on the back of my neck and arms to stand up. I believe if there were some on my feet they would have stood up, too. I must say in my defense, when I believe something has come from God's Word, I will take a stand defending it until proven wrong. After the woman led prayer in the presence of men, (this was not good according to my teaching at that time. I was so wrong and judgmental). I immediately approached the host who had organized the event and said that I would not be a part of any event that had a woman that called herself a pastor as a co-sponsor. I told them either she goes, or I would go. Since it was clear that I was very serious (I was the major sponsor) she was asked to back out. Lord, I never knew that woman's name, yet I have prayed for forgiveness so many times. I pray one day that I will be able to tell her face to face. Even that old Baptist church I used to attend now has a female assistant pastor. Further, here I stand now ready to proclaim and preach of God's glory to any that will listen. Lord, I thank you for revealing the truth of Your Word to me.

Chapter Fifteen

I was riding high. I felt I had finally arrived. I was somebody. People knew me on the street, and I had money in my pockets. I thought I was grounded, and nothing had changed about me other than my success. I continued to help people and attend church. I had always taken pride in whatever I did so what was the problem? I was soon to find out.

While building my career, I never took the time to divorce my alcoholic husband. It didn't take him long to find out how I fared in his absence. One day he just showed up at the beauty college. My secretary burst into my office and told me a man was out in the front lobby yelling that this was his G ___ D _____ school. No one knew I was married so she did not know what to think. I was as surprised to see him as they were. His first words to me were, "Honey, I'm home."

I made it perfectly clear he didn't have a home with me or anything I had. He was sober and was easy to reason with in the past while sober. He hadn't drunk in years, and I prayed that he was old enough to make a change and move on with his life without me. Wrong!!!

My television program was broadcast live because I took questions on the air from callers. The calls were filtered, however he managed to get through to me. Before he could be disconnected, he slurred obscenities and threats against myself, the college and my salon. I was totally humiliated.

After that everything started to go downhill. The enrollment at the school dropped due to transfers to other facilities and several weeks went by without new entries. I was asked to withdraw as host of the television show and radio spots. Although I had managed to save some money, I did not anticipate the quick drop in the income from the college. With constant surprise visits from my estranged husband the stylists at the salon did not feel safe and soon found booths at other salons located in the area. My financial empire was crumbling around me.

It didn't take long once it was established that our relationship was over for him to consult lawyers. I was so naive not to have filed for divorce. To my dismay I learned that he was entitled to half of everything that I acquired. He had caused severe damage to my income but there was still value in the equipment and supplies.

Without consulting the Lord in what I should do I started making plans to liquidate everything and move away from the problem. Fear took over me. I shut down everything and moved to Alabama. Aletha had gotten married and started a family of her own. Two months after the move my divorce was final and eight months later my ex-husband died from an infection in a tooth that filtered throughout his body.

Chapter Sixteen

⁓

The first week I moved to Daphne, AL. I found a new church home. It had been a long time since I felt at home in a place of worship. Pastor Drake and Becky were the first white preachers that I ever had as spiritual leaders. God will bring people into your life for a special season. The two of them were different. Different in every way. The music was different, the predominately white congregation was different, and the worship service was even stranger to me. I watched services like these on TV while watching Oral Roberts with Big Mama. But I had never heard people actually speaking in tongues or falling out in the floor after having been prayed over. It was foreign to me. All of these new things were confusing and caused me to ask many questions. Sometimes those questions made me more confused, but I knew I wanted more understanding of God's Word and simply more God in my life. Pastor Drake's teaching manner of preaching was just what I needed. He took time to explain the answers to my questions and when I would get frustrated because it just didn't fit with what I had been taught in the past, he would be patient with me. I was stubborn in my acceptance of this new way to serve God. As hard as I tried, I did not get it. I needed to see it in the Bible before I could accept it. The principle of that teaching came from my first mentor that I loved and respected Pastor Hoover. I was a believer and even the devil believes that there is a God but does the believer have faith in God? I knew that God existed. I believed in Him, and I was willing to submit to his will.

I moved a week after Adrian graduated high school to Daphne, MS. I enrolled Angela at Daphne High school, and I became completely engulfed with making sure that my two girls were secure in their new environment. This was when my last daughter entered my life. LaToya came home with Angela from school and it's like she never left. Come to find out she was having an extremely difficult and troubling home life. To keep it simple her mom gave her over to me. She was young and had a darling little girl named Destiny then soon after LaDarius was born. She became part of my family both emotionally and legally. She says that I saved her life but in reality, I was broken and so was she. It took God bringing us together to mend us both.

Everything was going well until I fell into the old pattern of needing someone to fill my void of not having a soulmate. I continued to long to have a good marriage. With everything that happened in my life I felt like I was a failure. My brother Toby was the smart one. He was Valedictorian of his class. He was physically talented and had a promising future in basketball. After he graduated, he started his career in engineering. Avis was a MISTER personality. Plus, he also had a very good job in engineering. I felt like I was just Mom's illegitimate child that couldn't seem to stay in a decent relationship. I was continuing to fail in life. I was living life through my children, which was fine at first, then came Ricky.

He was a tall, good-looking man with blue eyes. Even his family was confused on whether they were White or Black. His dad said they were Black, but his grandfather said White. Ricky wasn't sure either way, but he looked White. They honestly had half their family buried in a White cemetery and the other half buried in the Black cemetery. You would think with the uncertainty of his heritage that would make it easy for our relationship, but the reality of the South made it extremely difficult for us. We couldn't go to restaurants without stares and glares from both races. With the troubles and conflicts of today's society, marriage with teenage daughters and him being unsaved, I knew in my heart I should have never gotten involved. I thought I could change him. I would basically threaten him with my not wanting to be involved with anyone who wasn't saved or didn't attend church. As a result, he would try to please me. But we argued regularly about going to church to Bible study and Sunday services. It was as if I had to drag him to do what I thought should be natural.

I decided to take a job in a food restaurant. I didn't want Ricky to carry the burden of the household and my teenage daughters. Soon after I slipped and fell on the job. For months I was in treatment and sent to doctors. Eventually, one specialist placed her hands on my knee and told me, "I'm sorry to tell you this, but I believe that you have multiple myeloma." I said, "Okay." She explained further, "No you don't understand this could be a fatal condition."

I had no idea about the disease. She set up an appointment for me to see a specialist the following week. When I drove into the parking lot, I saw something that said cancer unit at the end of the building. I took Angela with me. I said, "Angela I believe they're trying to tell me that I have cancer." She said, "No you have to go back to the other side of the building downstairs." However, I had to take the elevator up to the fourth floor and when the elevator doors opened there was a big sign above the information desk that said Cancer Unit. That was how I found out I was being tested for cancer.

The workman's compensation stopped the same week the doctor reported the cancer diagnosis. All my benefits from the job were cut off. Things got tougher and I had to apply for SSI. With the diagnosis I was approved for an immediate six months short term disability. It was just enough for them to confirm the diagnosis and explain what needed to be done. At the end of the six months once again I was cut off with no benefits. I still needed medications and treatments. For the first time my children's money from their jobs mattered. Before I was diagnosed, they were asked to give $25 out of their checks to simply teach them responsibility. Now they were supporting me. The doctors that I could get to see me started medicating me with lots of opioids, morphine and muscle relaxers. They were so strong, it got to the point where I would sleep all the time, and actually lost track of time and days. My oncologist scheduled a double biopsy for me to check my levels because I had been on the medications for so long. I was told the medication and anesthesia did not affect me as it should.

I felt the pain as she chipped bone from my pelvis area. She asked if I would like to stop but I knew that would be the only way that we could get the results that were needed for my treatment. It was late evening when I was released from the clinic and the doctor had forgotten to give me my prescriptions for pain. When the nerves became completely active again, I was in extreme pain and my daughters went back to the facility to get the prescriptions that I needed. It was after hours, and the doctor was already gone.

Knowing that I was in pain I'm sure that my daughters tried to get in contact with everyone that they possibly could to get me some relief. The next day I got a phone call from the doctor's office stating that I would no longer be able to attend the clinic because my children had come soliciting drugs. That was my wake-up call. I felt that I was addicted to the doctor-prescribed medications. I called Pastor Drake and got some scriptures from him for healing and told him that I was going to stop taking the drugs. I stopped cold turkey. I felt like a drug addict on the street. For four long days I went through sweats, vomiting, hallucinations and extreme pain. I started off strong in my faith. Quoting scripture out loud to myself. But as the pain and anxiety got extremely worse, I stopped reading my Bible and I threw it across the room.

After a few moments I would go back and pick it up and read more scriptures. I did that about four times while going through withdrawals.

I made a promise to God that if I got through the withdrawals whenever I had another pain I would pray and ask Him to take it away or make the pain subside.

Surprisingly, once I got off the medication I actually started to feel better. I started trying to work toward getting my strength and doing more things. All three of my girls were enrolled in college and were studying to become medical assistants. My oldest daughter remained in Indiana and was married with a family of her own. The social pressure was already getting to Ricky. I guess the complications of my illness were too much for him to bear and one day he went to work and simply didn't come home.

I finally took some time to look at myself. I needed to figure out why this was continually happening to me. Was I the cause of my latest dark episode? What was I doing that was making me repeat the same patterns over and over again? I was determined to get off the crazy merry-go-round that I was riding. I accomplished the first stage to change which was to recognize that I had problems and I did have problems. The second stage was harder. I had to take accountability for my actions.

In hindsight it was sadly apparent that I developed a pattern of making rash decisions when things were tough. Frankly, I would run or take the easy way out. I didn't have a foundation sturdy enough to stay put. I thought I believed and was living according to God's Word. Yes, I guess I was what you would call a religious person. I had some Christian values, but I really wasn't a student of the Word of God. I knew from some Bible studies that there were promises and good things for believers, but I did not know why I wasn't getting them or even experiencing the joy of the Lord in my life.

I made a conscious decision to start studying and reading the Bible and more importantly not to be self-taught. I wanted to learn how to get a correct understanding of the scriptures. Being under the ministry of Pastor Drake was the beginning of the process.

James 1:22-25

22 But be doers of the word, and not hearers only, deceiving yourselves.

23 For if anyone is a hearer of the word and not a doer, he is like a man who looks intently at his natural face in a mirror.

24 For he looks at himself and goes away and at once forgets what he was like.

25 But the one who looks into the perfect law, the law of liberty, and perseveres, being no hearer who forgets but a doer who acts, he will be blessed in his doing.

I accomplished many things and did some good works, but they weren't with the right intent of the heart. My purpose in those times was to impress others, mainly my mother and family. I even wanted to impress my biological father to show him that I made something of my life in spite of him not being in my life. Lastly, I needed to prove to myself that I had value and could be successful. Looking back, I was so full of myself. I was so proud and puffed up about what I did. I, me, Ms. Connie.

That was the beginning of my downfall. I had not given God enough credit. Nor was I a good steward of what He had blessed me with. In my adolescence I learned to depend on my stepfather for my support. He was my support at that time but in my adult years I felt there was no one for me to lean on. Instead of turning to God for the encouragement and support that I needed when things got bad, I would run away or put my trust in a man who was unstable himself. When all else failed I would hide in the darkness taking my pain along with me, isolating myself from spiritual guidance.

Chapter Seventeen

~

While in the absence of a man in my life, spiritually I was getting on the right track but financially I was falling apart. The savings were gone and so was Ricky. I had no choice but to try to find another job. My cosmetology licenses expired but I took the regular and instructor's written tests for Alabama. Of course, I passed them both because I had taught the course for 20 plus years. I got a job at a salon but with all the medical bills I barely kept things going. One Saturday morning another stylist asked me to go get lunch with her at the club down the street. To my surprise the place was full for that time of day. Several men were making passes, but I had sworn off any relationship with a man and was working on being able to be alone and self-sufficient with the help of the Lord. Suddenly, my friend almost pushed me off my seat and told me to switch chairs with her because the man next to her was worrying her to death about me.

Matthew was a well-dressed ruggedly handsome man with straight curly hair and Indian features. He was tall and cut like an Adonis figurine.

When he spoke, his voice was so deep it boomed across the room. I thought the devil was setting me up by putting everything I liked out on a table before me. But this time I was on my best defense. I wasn't giving out my number. I didn't care how much he begged. Finally, my friend said let's go but promised him that she would bring me back later that evening because I was riding with her. After I refused to give out my number again, he told me that he was going to be waiting for me.

Sherri and I actually blew off work that evening. It was the first time I had done anything since getting ill and being abandoned by Ricky. When we arrived back at the social club late that evening, I decided not to stay and headed towards my car. Matthew followed me out and asked why I was leaving. I explained that I stopped going to clubs and didn't go out much. I let him know I wasn't interested in dating at the moment. He gave me the usual line that he wasn't really into clubbing either. He quickly wrote down his number and told me to call him so he would know I made it home safely. Once home I picked up the phone and put it back down about three times before I made the call. I don't know what happened, but we had a really good conversation. When he asked me, "Why are you choosing to live your life alone because you are too young and pretty to give up." I think I experienced a meltdown because everything poured out. All the hurt and pain from the past relationships came out with a waterfall of tears and emotion. It should have been enough to make any man or woman hang up the phone. Instead, he listened and tried to console me over the phone until I stopped crying. He told me, "I just want to be there for you if you let me." The phone call ended with him stating that he would meet me at my church the next day. This was the beginning of our friendship. I was still having some health issues. Finances were still strained but beginning to get better. Matthew would come by each payday and give me money to help although I never asked for his assistance.

He also started attending church with me and the girls. I was still screaming, "I don't want a man in my life," but Matthew was persistent. It was Matthew's decision for us to get our lives in order and get married, not simply live together.

Proverbs 18:22

"He who finds a wife finds a good thing and obtains favor from the Lord."

This time I waited, and someone chose me. I didn't try to force love and I really tried my best to repel it. I even told my girls that he was too old for me, even though he was only two years older than me.

I didn't have to convince him or coax him to become close to God, he wanted it for it himself. He was honest and told me his shortcoming was that he wasn't well-educated but good old common sense and people skills made up for any shortcoming he might have had.

He, too, had survived bad marriages. Although he wasn't a strong believer, he had the desire to want to grow and was willing to listen and to learn about living a Christian life. He had a kind and gentle spirit. Because we were both open and honest when we first met, we knew each other's struggles and were both determined to work together and let God lead in our relationship. We vowed not to give up or walk away once married. Matthew was a good provider and hard worker. However, shortly after we were married, he also became ill and had to apply for disability. The process took two years. Financially it was hard, but my spiritual life grew immensely through the struggles.

Pastor Drake would have guest speakers come in from time to time. There was a young lady who was in the Army that survived some form of cancer, and she was speaking about how she was healed and how God gave her a testimony. I was really impressed by what she said and the way she spoke. I guess I looked up to her.

It was around Thanksgiving and the church was giving out Thanksgiving baskets. She and the secretary showed up at my door with the basket. When she asked me what was going on with my treatment, I said I didn't know because I had to have some more tests. She said if I was that sick, I should have a team of doctors. It was more the way she said it than what was said. Her words immediately threw me off balance. They stabbed me like a knife. I really wanted to scream, "I don't have VA insurance benefits!" You don't get a team of doctors, nor could I even get scheduled to get the tests that I needed because the hospital would not schedule me without having insurance.

My heart sank while she was speaking to me. Or was it the devil making me think that she thought I wasn't sick at all? It crushed me. Here I was trying to follow the guidelines of what I was being taught. Walking as though I had received my healing. Not speaking words that announced how much physical pain I was in and continuing to go to church. And the one I listened to the most was judging me for doing a good job of faking it until I made it. Instead of responding or asking more questions to give her a chance to explain her words, I turned around and walked back in the house and broke down in tears. Again, I turned the situation into church hurt. I pulled away and stopped attending the church. My emotional state of mind went with me, and I also left any form of spiritual guidance behind me. I did not explain to Pastor Drake why I left the church until years later. I had succumbed once again to the devil's game. I allowed him to isolate me from God. My children and I were growing under the teaching. I allowed my feelings to get me out of position to grow closer to God. The devil stepped in between us blocking God's light. My emotions were telling me everything negative about what she said. But could it have been that she had never been without medical insurance to know of the trials and tribulations that were going on in my life. I didn't take the time to explain. Instead, I allowed the devil to take control. My season under leadership with Pastor Drake had ended but he taught me the importance of using scriptures that referred to the promises you're asking God for when you pray.

I also learned not to put my trust or beliefs in a human whether male or female, pastor or bench warmer. My trust must remain in God and God's Word. I made a promise to myself that I would not leave a church where the Word of God is preached unless moved by God.

Chapter Eighteen

Even in the worst of times we never lived in the slums or became homeless. Somehow God always managed to keep a roof over our heads, and we were still truly blessed to not have to live on the streets. There were times when we came close, but God...

When Hurricane Ivan entered the Gulf region, we were living in a house in Mobile, AL. We were still in financial straits and on the verge of getting evicted. I already filed for bankruptcy. I was a little healthier at the time but not at my best.

Something in my spirit kept telling me to purchase renter's insurance. We never really experienced a hurricane and I didn't know what to expect. I started calling insurance companies that morning. Everyone that I was calling told me that the storm was already in the area, and they weren't taking any more applications. Finally, about 2:30 that afternoon I reached a company that was accepting applications for renter's insurance. The cost to get started was $35. When I asked how I could get the payment to them since they did not take payment over the phone, to my surprise they were located a short distance from my home but with the way the streets were set up in the neighborhood with the cut-off of the blocks and going around fencing it was more like a 10-block walk. I didn't have a car at the time and Matthew was at work. She said the cost to get the policy started would be $35.

I only had $40 cash on hand. I was debating with myself whether to keep the funds for food or other needs after the storm or follow the voice telling me to purchase the insurance. I got out of bed, got dressed then started the walk to the building. Since I was in bed for a while and not able to do a lot of exercise or moving around, I was quite exhausted from the walk. When I got there, the agent told me she did not take cash, only a bank card which made my heart sink. I walked another 10 blocks to my daughter Angela's job to have her use her debit card. She went with me back to the insurance office. After I finished the required paperwork when Angela and I stepped out the door, I actually fainted and fell in the doorway.

It started to rain. The insurance company was about to close so the agent helped me up and offered us a ride home.

The hurricane was due to hit the next day. We spent the hours during the hurricane in the center hallway with mattresses against the walls. We heard several loud crashes before the lights went out. After the storm was over, we went outside to check on the house and we found a large tree on the east side of the house had fallen. Another tree fell directly in front of the house blocking the front door and the third tree fell on the west side of the house disconnecting the power box from the house. A spark occurred as a result and started as a small electrical fire in the kitchen, which we were able to put out, but it caused a lot of smoke damage within the house. Two of my daughters have a history of severe asthma, so the insurance company replaced all the furniture, clothing and relocated us into a hotel for three months. Finally, we were given the option to relocate into another house before the benefits expired. The $35 payment and making the 20-block walk resulted in $86,000 and stability for my family.

I can truly say God loved me enough that he used a hurricane to save me. Through prayer and trust in God, I learned I could depend on God and to move when He tells you. I could have held on to the $40 and stayed in bed worrying about the storm and how I would survive but I place my faith in God not the insurance company but my true provider, Jehovah Jirah.

Chapter Nineteen

After being reestablished, we still remained disconnected from a church home. I was walking for exercise around my house when I met a lady named Eloise. She invited me to her church and so began my season under the ministry of Bishop David & Margaret Richie.

Gulf Coast Christian Center Ministries was very active in the community. Soon my children and I were very active members of the church. One of the strong points of the church was the Bible study and prayer meetings. Pastor Margaret was very caring and sincerely cared for the members of the church. We developed a very good relationship. I could call and speak with her and Pastor David on an almost daily basis. I became part of the Intercessory Ministry. Members would meet on Tuesday and Thursday morning at 6 am and pray before going to our daily jobs or activities. During this time, we prayed for the needs of the church family, community and any other problem that was brought before us.

I witnessed first-hand the results of prayers being lifted up. People were healed, financial needs met, and the favor of God was abundant. Through my prayers my faith was increased.

I truly began to understand prayer and faith go hand-in-hand. More importantly, the only way to strengthen your faith is to believe, trust and watch God bring it to fruition. When you experience it for yourself no one can make you have doubts. Faith increases through trials and tribulation; experiencing the outcome of God's grace and mercies. Faith is put into action by praying to God with the belief that it is already done. Doubt counteracts faith and delays or cause blessings to be blocked.

2 Corinthians 5:7 (NIV)
"For we walk by faith, not by sight."

It is natural to fear. Everyone has fears, but it's how you deal with the fear that will prove your growth and your faith in God. Matthew and I had been married for seven years at this point. We were living in a large, very nice home in Mobile. My girls finished the medical assistant program and started a billing and coding class. They were at the end of their training but still living at home. LaToya had given birth to two other children, LaDarrein and DeAsia. We had a house full of love. We had our three younger daughters and my four grandchildren. Everyone did their part and we operated as a village providing emotional and financial support for each. For several years I kept my promise to God not to rely on pain medication. I did not realize how faithful he was to me until I experienced pain mostly at night. When I laid down it was extremely painful. I developed a ritual where I would pray asking the Lord to take away the pain. In a few moments it would subside, and I would go to sleep. I did this for several months until one day Matthew insisted that I go to the hospital to get it checked. At the emergency room the doctor gave me an x-ray and told me, "Well, the problem is you're constipated." I could see these big balls of what he called "stool" on the x-ray. I was prescribed a stool softener and told to go home, and I would be okay.

I was already scheduled for my regular doctor's appointment two days later. When I got to the doctor, I explained to him what was going on and he sent me across the street from his office to another hospital in Fairhope, AL. I was given a sonogram, and after the test I knew I was in trouble when the radiologist came in and asked me if I could walk. I said, "Yes, of course I'm fine to walk." She asked if, I was sure. I said yes and she sternly told me to go back across the street. She said, "Do not go home. Your doctor will be getting the results and waiting."

This was one of the few times I had gone to the doctor's office by myself. My doctor had the report in his hand when I walked through the door. He said, "You cannot go home. I don't know why they let you leave. I am going to admit you to the hospital. Your gallbladder has ruptured." He explained that what the other physician had diagnosed as stool was actually large, golf ball-sized gallstones throughout my stomach.

Emergency surgery was performed on me before my family could even arrive at the hospital. The surgery took more than five hours. The surgeon explained to my mother and family that I was within hours from dying. My gallbladder was in such terrible condition that it was like rotten tissue ripping apart. Gangrene had spread throughout my stomach area as a result I had abscesses on my kidney and on the top part of my liver. After the first surgery two days later, I had to go back to have the abscess removed from the liver. The doctor said it was the worst case that he had ever experienced, and I was very lucky to be alive. I explained that it was not luck, it was God. He asked how I had endured the pain and of course that brought back to my memory my prayer to God. God had allowed me not to experience excruciating pain because of my belief and faith in him. I experienced what I requested of Him. His grace and his mercy sustained me long enough for me to become aware that it was He who sustained me.

Chapter Twenty

Once I recovered, I returned to my post of intercessory prayer Warrior. The early morning prayer services and Sunday services encouraged me during the week. It gave me hope that God would provide regardless of what it looked like.

God showed me again that He was with me because the medical bills kept coming but somehow one way or another my needs were being met.

On one occasion I received an electrical bill for termination of service. I didn't have the money and I exhausted every avenue that I had to borrow any type of funds to keep the services on. I spoke with the supervisors explaining that I had my grandbabies in the house, and it was winter. But I could not get any assistance. I got up early that morning and went to the prayer service as usual. Pastor Margaret and my friend Eloise were there. I started to cry out and pray with everything within me at the altar.

I started reciting the promises of God for His children. I spoke that I would be a lender not a borrower and my needs would be met. Eloise and Pastor Margaret joined prayer in agreement for my request. ***Ephesians 6:18-20 (NIV) "18And pray in the Spirit on all occasions with all kinds of prayers and requests. With this in mind, be alert and always keep on praying for all the Lord's people. 19Pray also for me, that whenever I speak, words may be given me so that I will fearlessly make known the mystery of the gospel, 20for which I am an ambassador in chains."*** During the prayer session, it came back to my memory that Social Security had been taking out Medicare insurance payments for months and I was told the money was going to be refunded. The prayer sessions normally only lasted one hour. It was going on at 7:00am and service to my house was due to be turned off first thing that morning. I explained to the prayer warriors that I was going to make a phone call to the Social Security office and drive to the electric company to be there when it opened.

When I left the church, Eloise was on a three-way call with me while I waited on hold for the Social Security office. When I entered the electric company, it just so happened that the department supervisor walked into the office as soon as I started speaking to the representative. The representative from the Social Security office came on the line at the same time. I had her on speakerphone as I explained to the electric company agent that I didn't have the funds but was due a refund from Social Security. I asked the electric company supervisor if they would wait until the refund came in the mail.

After the Social Security officer heard what was happening, she said that she would order the check to be printed immediately and I should have it by the end of the week. Once they heard that, the supervisor of the electronic company agreed to keep my lights on until I received the check. The supervisor asked how much the refund was. The Social Security officer responded and said $875.67. The electric company representative turned pale in the face and handed me the cut off notice and announced the amount needed was $875.64. It was three pennies less than the cost of the bill. When Eloise (who was silently listening) heard that; she screamed and started speaking in tongues.

The two supervisors in the office, the Social Security representative and I all had a hallelujah good time for a couple of minutes. God had answered my prayer in a way that proved he moved on my behalf. Again, the number 3 stood out in coming to my rescue. Was it just coincidental or representative of the Trinity? I chose to believe it was the latter: the Father, the Son and the Holy Spirit. The electric company's supervisor's appearance at that moment did not happen by chance. The fact that I got a representative in the Social Security office who was willing and able to process the refund alone was a miracle. God placed into motion the answer to my prayer months before I asked. Matthew and I would not have set aside the funds needed earlier because there was always something that our money had to go to as soon as it hit the bank. There were things the girls needed as well as taking care of things at the house. I believed that God would provide but faith without action is dead. When I started the drive to the electric company with the Social Security office on hold, I made a step in faith.

I didn't know how much the check was for or if it could be released or even if the power company would wait for payment. But I knew if it was going to be done God would have to do it. I thanked God for His favor, grace, and mercy.

In the midst of everything else, one morning while in the bathroom I combed my hair and noticed strands of hair falling out. I started screaming and crying so loudly that my daughters Adrian, Angela and LaToya came running to the bathroom. When they asked me what was wrong, I looked at them horrified and said, "My hair is falling out in patches." They all looked at each other and burst out laughing. I asked what was so funny. They all said at the same time, "Mom, you cut your hair off all the time. Half the time you wear a boys' cut." I said, "Yeah, but this is different because I wanted to do it then." In the end I took out the clippers and cut it down real low. I threw on one of my many wigs and we started laughing. So, when I went bald no one ever found out that I lost all my hair.

Chapter Twenty-One

I continued to struggle with health issues with chronic back pain and a blood disorder. On numerous occasions I was told my condition was so severe, and I could possibly die. After having many episodes like this I came home and told my girls the doctor said that my condition was extremely bad. They simply said, "Okay, Mom." To my surprise they continued with their plans for the day and were about to walk out the door. I looked at them and started crying. They asked, "Mom, what's the matter?"

I said, "I'm telling you the doctor said I might possibly die and y'all just walking out the door." Again, my children looked at each other and one of them said, "Mom, you always tell us it's going to be okay. We are to pray and act as though it's already done. We have faith in God, and it always turns out alright! We're just doing what you told us to do."

I was dumbfounded. My children were correcting me. I realized that they were watching and experiencing growth in faith with me. We had watched together how God came through time and time again.

The next day they got up and came into the bedroom and asked me, "What are we doing today?" I looked up and smiled. I said, "Y'all going to get out of my face. I'm okay now. Yes, I had a 10% moment, but I got up and I am going to keep going. Gods got this." Adrian being her usual self said, "Well, are we believing it today or not? Can we leave or do we need to stay?" We all laughed, and I put them out of my room.

Chapter Twenty-Two

After we relocated things seemed to calm down a lot. We became more financially stable, and my health issues seemed to subside somewhat. I was complacent with just simply sitting at home doing nothing. Both Matt and I were receiving disability and my children had jobs and were contributing to the household as well. I started to get that old feeling again. This time I prayed and asked God to show me the purpose for my life. Why was I down here in the south with nothing to do? Yes, I went to church and was part of the intercessory prayer team and I took care of my household, but I felt like something was missing in my life.

In 2011, my brother Avis called me. He was managing a steel mill company just outside of Bay St. Louis, Mississippi. I was still living in my home in Mobile at the time. He said he had a young gentleman that was working for him that wanted to open a beauty supply. He asked if I would come and give him some advice on how to get it started. I told him I would be happy to help him.

I drove up and met with Lonnie Bradley and his friend Ricky Lewis. I helped him get vendors for his supplies to stock the shelves. I didn't ask for any money, but he gave me $45 each time I came to pay for my gas. People started asking me to do their hair when they would come in to pick up supplies. Eventually I set up a booth inside the supply store to do hair. I started getting so many people that I was able to open a salon right next door to the beauty supply store. The salon started doing fairly well and it gave me something to do. Matthew was happy because he loved to talk to people and there was always someone coming by the corner store in the small strip mall. Everyday there was a man that would ride his bicycle to the store, purchase a 40-oz of beer, and hang the clear plastic bag on the arms of his bicycle. He rode away only to come back an hour later and do the same thing again. Throughout the day other people would stand in front of the store and talk or hang out in their cars.

The drive back and forth from Waveland to Mobile got to be too much after a while. It was about an hour and a half drive to get there and to come back home. My girls were taking care of the house while I was gone. In the back of the salon there was a closet. There was a shelf in it, probably 6 feet long and about 3 feet wide. Matthew and I would stack pillows on the counter and sleep on that shelf. Matthew just kept saying, "If you are here with me, I don't care where we sleep." God truly blessed me with a man that was selfless and not afraid to allow me to do what made me happy.

We started off going back to Mobile on Thursday nights for Bible study and driving back the next morning to work at the shop. We would return to Mobile for church on Sunday.

Chapter Twenty-Three

The area in Bay St. Louis was called the hood. To me it was bad enough to be called a hood. It was not ghetto fabulous, but it was an area where people normally congregated in the streets and simply hung out talking. I started noticing that people didn't seem to have any direction. They were just hanging out and doing nothing with their lives.

One day while braiding a young man's hair, he received a phone call from someone in jail. Before he ended the call, they passed the phone to six other people that were either family members or friends in the jail. The customer, David, laughed and thought it was funny, but it really upset my spirit to the point that I found myself continually speaking on it. Finally, one night I heard a voice tell me, "If you're not going to do anything about it then stop talking about it." Somehow, I knew it was the Lord. This time I prayed and asked Him for guidance as to what I could do to help the situation in the community.

Of course, I had to do what I have been doing for years. Teaching was what I knew best and teaching in the hair industry had been my most successful career. That is how I started the quest to open a cosmetology school in Mississippi.

I did all the research for what would be available to help with the startup cost and the financial aid for my prospective students. After getting the requirements needed for a cosmetology school, I found out the size of the building and the amount of equipment would be way too costly. However, opening a barber school and equipment didn't require as much space. The first problem was that I had to convert my cosmetology license to a barber license and then apply for the instructor's license in order to be able to open the school. I felt this was what God wanted me to do so I did what was necessary to successfully acquire licenses. I closed the salon and moved a few blocks down the street to a larger building.

Unfortunately, once in the building I found out all the promises made to me for funding were not true. There wouldn't be any funding available for my students until after the school had been successful in business for two years. The only money available was enough to fund employing a secretary for the business, and a percentage would be retro paid. Despite the setbacks, I still continued to work on the vision. I felt confident that God had given me the vision and that he would provide what was necessary in order for it to come to fruition.

Chapter Twenty-Four

There was a young man who would come to the shop every other week to get his hair cut at the shop. While he was there, he and I would engage in some very high-spirited conversations about the Bible to the point that I really enjoyed having discussions with him when he came into the shop. He seemed to have a knowledge of the Bible above his years. After almost a year he told me that he was a pastor, and he was in the process of building his church. He showed me the blueprints of a frame of the building that they started. He said that he was currently holding services in a hall in Gulfport. I explained my church home was still in Mobile and we drove back and forth each Sunday. Pastor Preston told me if one Sunday, I couldn't make it to my church to come visit him.

I was struggling and it seemed as though I was trying to do everything right. I was trying to live according to what I knew of God's Word, but it felt like everybody was getting blessed except me. Why did I lose everything? Matthew and I graduated from sleeping on the shelf to a blow-up mattress that we pulled out and rolled up every morning. I knew some of what happened was my fault, but I wanted to know why I could not experience joy or build an inheritance for my children and keep it. I prayed for the Lord to give me some answers or some peace of mind that I was in his will.

That next Sunday I visited the hall where Pastor Preston was preaching. He delivered a sermon that was direct affirmation from God. Not only did it bless my soul, but it corrected a misinterpreted scripture in which I was very familiar.

James 1:2-3 (NKJV)

"2 My brethren, count it all joy when you fall into various trials,

3 knowing that the testing of your faith produces [a]patience."

Count it all joy. He explained that a lot of people believe that the word count in the context refers to numbers like 1, 2, 3... that we are to count the situation joyful. But this definition for the word count in that scripture refers to being a Duke, ruler or governor. In other words, I am the governor of my joy. I am in control of my joy. I'm not to allow the devil or my emotions to take over how I feel no matter what the situation looks like but to be assured in the fact I have hope in God and that He is in control.

That message provided me with the spiritual food that I needed, and I shared the message over and over with a number of people that I have met since. I attended Pastor Preston's church for several months thereafter, and finally met with Bishop Richie to inform him I was considering changing my membership to Perfect Peace Christian Ministries under the leadership of Pastor Torien Preston. I wanted to leave a church for the first time decent and in order. The Richie's and my church family at GCCM had been good to me and for me and my family. Bishop Richie and Pastor Margaret gave me their blessings. Pastor Margaret said that she felt that my starting the school was an extension of their ministry and actually presented me with the framed picture that their spiritual leaders had given them when they set out to start a ministry in Mobile. To this day that picture hangs inside the school building.

Chapter Twenty-Five

After getting things in order in the building it was brought to my attention by a neighbor that the building was in the paper because the landlord was in foreclosure. I was back to ground zero.

I located another building in the sister city of Waveland, MS. I mentioned the changes that needed to be made to the building to Pastor Preston. After I returned from signing the papers, I drove up to the building to see Bishop Preston with a team of young men pulling up carpet. Even though his own church was not complete, he took the time to help me. We sat at tables and had Bible study in the building that evening.

Things began to work in my favor. On April 13, 2013, Unique Transitions Training Center, LLC was approved as a barber college. I was informed by the president of the Barber Board that I was the first Afro-American female to own a barber college in the state of Mississippi.

At that time, I also became the city of Waveland's only Black-owned licensed business. Although I was proud of the accomplishments it bought about a lot of barriers and racial prejudices. I soon found out that a lot of programs for which I applied either got lost until the deadlines had passed or blatantly denied.

All of the young men and women in the area who had an interest in the hair industry without being licensed, enrolled in my school. Since the students were cutting in the community before the school was established, they had a clientele which came with them. The school was in a building connected to the landlord's insurance company. This turned out to be a pain in my side literally. Although I had strict rules and regulations which included no loitering, no sagging pants or profanity of any kind inside or outside of the building there were always complaints from the owner. I was told that when two or more of my students took a 10-minute break in front of the building that it scared away his older, white female customers. I had to limit and monitor when my students could come and go in order to keep the peace. Finally, I made them take cigarette breaks in the back of the building.

Despite those few negative problems, the school was thriving financially and developed a reputation for having well-trained students. The community was accepting of the business, but I was still in the South and the "good ole boy" system which was in control of the purse strings was held closed to me.

I refused to lose track of my purpose for establishing the school. Just like a preacher has his church, my school became my pulpit. The music was gospel, and the atmosphere was filled with Christian motivation and inspirational scripture throughout. Of course, the majority of my students came a little rough around the edges but learned to respect the morals and conduct that I required for the business. They may have come for an education about hair care, but they also received a little knowledge about the goodness of the Lord free of charge. Some visited with me at church, and a few received the Lord as their personal Savior. With the cost of the rent for the building Matthew and I still could not afford an apartment. We bought a sleeper sofa for the lounge area and at night after we closed, we would pull it out to sleep. That being said, having reached even one soul and making a difference in their lives made the sacrifice so worthwhile. I praise God continuously for the opportunity to have been a small part of their lives. The first graduation of the Unique Transitions Training Center was held in September 2013. For some it was their first formal event. It was a full cap and gown ceremony.

I wish that I could say that everything was happily ever after but that's not the way the story goes. One busy evening a gentleman finished getting his haircut and walked outside the building to leave. There was an altercation with another gentleman who saw his car in the parking lot. There were shots fired. Although my school was not directly involved at all, the fact that it was the parking lot connected to my school brought negative attention. The newspapers played it up as if it happened inside the school. With the already strained relationship the owners filed to have me evicted from the property.

I fought for the reputation of my school in court when asked to pay for damages made to the building as a result of the incident. The judge ruled in my favor. To be on the safe side I looked for a new location. I stopped at a location at 501 Highway 90 that was a lumber company going out of business. There was a "For Sale" sign outside. When I went in and asked the owner how much he was selling it for he said he wanted $3 million dollars because of where it was located and the amount of land. I laughed and thanked him for his time.

Around the same time my two daughters who remained at the house in Mobile called me on a couple occasions telling me that they smelled a moldy type of odor in the house. They were both having trouble with their asthma, and when I went home, I was surprised to see black mold had covered just about everything from the furniture to the walls and ceilings. The pattern was a blackish color, too. The girls said they tried washing things down with bleach, but it came back.

I called a plumber who checked outside and under the house. He found out a pipe burst, and water was leaking like a river. The mold started growing underneath the house getting into the framework of the building. He told us we would have to move out of the house as it wasn't safe. The Board of Health ordered the homeowners to fix the problems before it could be rented or lived in again.

Almost everything that was cloth or fabric had to be disposed of because of the girl's asthma. Solid wood furniture and mattresses that were covered with plastic were the only things that we were able to take. We loaded everything on the moving truck to take to the storage that night, but it was late, and the movers emptied the truck the next morning. All of my valuables such as jewelry dishes and things of value were placed in the front room to be picked up for the next load. Unfortunately, during the night someone broke in and stole everything of value. All of my jewelry was gone and anything that was worth a quick dollar. They even stole the refrigerator out of the kitchen. This was the ultimate hurt. I felt as if I left my home to go to a city that didn't really want me there and end up losing everything I owned. I remember crying out, "Lord will I ever reap a harvest?" I downsized to a two-bedroom house for a short time. After a while the girls relocated Mississippi to help with the business.

Chapter Twenty-Six

Again, I was fortunate enough to find a location that was on the main highway, but it was positioned in the back of the plaza facing sideways. The unit was inside a large commercial building, so we were not allowed to sleep there overnight. I acquired a place for one week in Gulfport that did not work out in our best interest. On the last day of that week, I drove around the city praying as I drove. I said, "Lord, I don't want to live in an apartment. I don't want anyone living above me or on the side of me." I have heard horror stories about apartment living. But I told the Lord if it was His will for us to live in an apartment, we would.

Towards the end of the day, I passed a red sign at the end of a small apartment complex that said, "FOR RENT." I said to myself, "Okay, Lord I will call." When I asked the office manager if there were any efficiencies available, she said yes and she would meet me there to show it. I parked in front of one of the buildings and waited for her. I was still a little downhearted about having to settle for the apartment. When she got out of her car, I expected her to go into one of the buildings with townhouses. Instead, she walked to the center of the lot to a small building and opened it. It was once used as the office which had been converted to a one-bedroom apartment with a second room that had a full kitchen and space for a living room and dining room set. She said if I had come a week earlier it would not have been ready and she would have put me in a townhouse. God had already put into action an answer to my prayer. It was a stand-alone building with no one living above me or on the side of me. I still get chills every time I tell of how He blesses me with the desires of my heart. Business was steady but I needed to go to the next level. My wish was to network with other businesses in the community. I was told by one of the business owners that there would be a business luncheon with the Hancock Chamber of Commerce which was hosted monthly by different business owners. I wanted to host one in the hope that it would help me network and become more socially connected. When I asked the president of the organization if I would be able to host the event, she immediately told me no. Her explanation was,

"It costs a lot of money if that's what you want to do." I said, "Well, I'm pretty sure that I want to do it. What dates are open?" She said all the dates were taken and finally blatantly said no that I could not host the event.

When I got back to my shop, I thought about it and realized that I had just experienced racial prejudice at its best. First, she assumed that she knew what I had in my pocket to spend. (I consulted a couple of other businesses that were going to assist me.) Then she denied me a date or even an opportunity to do the same thing that other businesses were doing. When situations like this occurred before, I would have simply stayed quiet to keep the peace. I was tired of hearing the excuse that we lived in the South and there was nothing that could be done.

I made the decision that something needed to be done, so I went to the Hancock County Chamber area supervisors meeting and addressed the board. I didn't pull any punches. I told them about all of the unfair treatment I faced as a Black business owner. I still had records of the lost files and the denied applications that I placed timely and was qualified to receive. I was even told at one point that a supervisor of the WIN Job agency in Hancock County quit her job and took my application with her. Only mine. One board member actually came down from his seat and gave me his card in support. A few weeks later he was jumped and severely beaten. I don't know if the two were related but it sure makes me wonder.

Supers hear from barber college owner on fairness

BY CASSANDRA FAVRE
STAFF WRITER

The Hancock County Board of Supervisors on Monday heard from Constance Mims, owner of Unique Transitions Training Center, a barber college in Waveland.

Mims said she started her college seven years ago and did her "due diligence" by visiting agencies to explore funding opportunities for the college and students.

She said she's been everywhere from the mayors' offices to the Southern Mississippi Planning.

"The reason I'm here is that I want you to see me," Mims said. "It seems like every time I go and speak to one of these people, they'll say something to me to appease me. But then the moment I walk out, they forget about me or I evaporate."

● See OWNER/Page 8A

114

My appearance at the meeting made the newspapers and several people reached out to me and offered kind words but no leads on how to overcome my situation. As a result, I filed a $250,000 lawsuit against the Hancock County Chamber of Commerce. Although the lawsuit did not produce any money it did accomplish exactly what I needed. It brought attention to the blatant attempts to have the school financially fail. Once the media exposed that I kept a record of signed documents on everything when I reapplied the outcome was quite different.

I made alliances with white men in positions of power that were willing to speak on my behalf. Like my mother often said, a closed mouth doesn't get fed. Also, I finally realized coddling in the dark doesn't make your problems go away. They just fester until you blow up.

I submitted all the records and documents needed to get a small business loan and was told I would be approved. I found myself on the merry-go-round with a rented building once again. This time one of my clients told me while I was doing their hair that the strip mall was due to be foreclosed on in two days. The landlord picked up the payment the day before and said nothing.

Chapter Twenty-Seven

Within 5 years, I was able to acquire a lot of good salon equipment in hopes of adding a cosmetology school and a small daycare for my students while in my shop. Business was going well. Then a man came by the building in a business suit asking numerous questions. I was on my best behavior not to say anything negative and even dropped the suggestion that I could be the property manager for the new owner. The businessman said that he was checking things out for someone who might be interested in buying. I had become very good friends with Mayor Mike Smith. I called him and asked if he had heard anything about the building being sold. He said the same gentleman came to his office the other day and was the new owner. The mayor started suggesting properties for me because he knew of the struggle that I've had to endure to keep the business within the city. This time there were no tears in a panic. I didn't go to a pity party. I had come too far to give up. I recognized it was the devil setting me up; but it would be for a come up. I began to pray telling the Lord, He hadn't brought me this far to leave me. I knew it would work out one way or another. I knew by experience now if God gave me the vision, He would see it through to completion. I learned that whatever God requires of you He will give you what you need to accomplish it. I just needed to walk as though it were already done.

Regardless of the nice conversation I had with the new owner I received a 30-day eviction notice. All I could say was, "Lord, You have to make a way because I don't see my way out of this unending darkness. But I trust you." I said, "Lord, once again I am trying to provide an inheritance for my children and lift up Your name in this school so I need you to show up and show out so that all can see that you did this." Lastly, I prayed: "Lord, You gave this vision to me and everything that came with it. I leave it in your hands." That night I had the best sleep.

Chapter Twenty-Eight

The next day it was announced on television that the first person to die in Mississippi was a Black man named Howard Pickens who was a barber. Howard was a close friend, and his wife just finished my instructor's course. As a matter of fact, when I opened my first college, I was two barber chairs short of fulfilling the requirements for the approval of the college. Howard brought me two of the chairs out of his salon so I would be in compliance. Then the COVID-19 pandemic happened. All barber and non-essential businesses had to shut down. I was interviewed on television as a friend of Howard's. It showed me locking my doors to the business to close for the pandemic. The evictions could not be processed. I knew I was tired of not having ownership in the property where my business was located. I had no money. I mean zero dollars, but God told me to go search for a next place.

I went back to the large warehouse on 501 Highway 90 again. The building was empty. A woman's support thrift store was in the warehouse for about two years and then moved out. I hoped that if nothing else the owner would allow me to lease it. When I contacted the realtor Johanna, I was overjoyed to know she proudly proclaimed her faith in Christ Jesus. When I asked if the owner would consider leasing, she said no he wanted to sell it. I knew I couldn't come up with $3 million dollars, but I boldly asked what he would sell it to me for. Johanna said, "Let's pray about it and I will get with you tomorrow."

She called and I met her at the building. What she told me blew me away. She said the owner was following my history and liked what I was trying to do in the community, and he wanted me to have it. I was excited but still needed to know the price. She said he would sell it to me for only $500,000.00 with a down-payment of $15,000.00. Let me remind you again I had zero dollars in my pocket and no idea when the small business loan would be available. I was told it would take several weeks for everything to come together in order to go to closing on the building. There were no other options but to continue to trust in God and depend on His grace and mercies.

I took a deep breath and told Johanna to write up the offer for the purchase. The property was actually located on busy highway 90. It was a combination of three plots. The warehouse was actually a large building of over

9,000 square feet with a large parking lot facing the front of the building. The back was fenced with almost half a football field-size space behind it. There was another older building about the same size as the warehouse in the front. It was more than adequate space to relocate the barber college plus additional space to rent or lease. In order to have a smooth transition as there was a lot of remodeling that had to be done for the barber college relocation to be approved.

I didn't know how long the pandemic was going to last but I knew that my equipment could not remain in the building in case the eviction order was lifted. I asked for additional time for my property to be moved out of the building and promised that I would move as soon as I secured another building. To my surprise the new owner agreed. He evicted the tenants as he wanted to make some overdue repairs that the building needed, and it would take time to complete the project.

He said he could work around my units to give me the time I needed. The removal could not be put off indefinitely because the remodeling needed to be done before the moving of the heavy equipment could occur.

I explained my situation to the realtor. After consultation with the owner, she told me that no construction on the property could be done without a contract. She then asked me for one dollar which I gave her. A rental contract was drafted for one dollar for two months that allowed me to start the build out. So, the building was secured temporarily but I didn't know who I was going to get the remodeling done. First, I tried a handy man that tried to take advantage of my lack of knowledge of construction costs that didn't work out. Then, I called Lonnie Bradley who closed his beauty supply store a couple years before and was now buying and flipping homes. He and another couple of young men were working together on housing projects. Lonnie became like a son to me so when I called, he came to the building immediately. I didn't have the first idea about how to build the walls, run the plumbing or install two extra bathrooms.

As I said, the building was a lumber warehouse and the only place that had heat and air conditioning was in the two offices on the side of the large open room. There was a lot to get done with empty pockets. I thank God for his favor. Lonnie and his friends started bringing over supplies, and his contractors started doing work for little or nothing. I allowed them to store their extra supplies in the large building in the back and in return I was told I could use anything that I needed for my remodeling. Most of the construction was done by people who were recommended to me or folks that I assisted at one time or another. Lonnie stopped by regularly and kept an eye on the construction to make sure everything was going as it should.

I divided the building in half to have a professional shop on one side and the college on the other side. The warehouse ceilings were extremely high so I knew that the school would have a separate entrance way. There was also an entrance for the barbershop and salon. I was advised by the city that the partition between the two had to be halfway but must extend the full length of the building, which proved to be a problem later. The professional side was completed quickly. The barber college side required a lot more construction.

Two days before I was to close on the building, I still had not received my funds. I refused to cancel the scheduled meeting knowing one way or another God would come through. That evening the funds were deposited into my account and I was able to make the $15,000 down payment and pay closing costs. The purchase was complete and Unique Transitions Inc. had ownership of its location.

2020-03-25 16:11

With the pandemic came the disaster loans as well. Not only did I apply myself, but I helped others who needed assistance.

In turn I often was rewarded by them volunteering help or providing materials that l needed. I started a bartering system that eventually yielded a heating and air conditioning system for the building. Although the system was old and had to be revamped it was better than nothing.

After the ban for salons was lifted, I was ready for operation. I held the Grand Opening and graduation right in the front of the building. There was a good turn out and the mayor of Waveland, Mike Smith, spoke at the event. He acknowledged that I was the first Afro-American woman in Mississippi to solely own a barber school, and that I was the only Black business owner in the city of Waveland at that time. I immediately gave God the glory for all that had been accomplished. I knew by experience if it had not been for the Lord going before me and preparing the hearts and souls of others nothing could have been done.

I thank God for the people that he placed in my path in this community. When the hiccups seemed like mountains in my path people showed up to help me by dedicating their time, money, and efforts to make sure that the school was approved. Once the school was up and running, there was an inspection, and I was told the school could not officially open because the dividing wall did not go from the ceiling to the floor. Even though I explained my directions for the build out came directly from the barber board itself it did not matter. They shut me down immediately and gave me less than seven days to get the wall built.

All it took was one phone call and I had a team of workers from the community that came and worked night and day to get the wall built and complete everything that was required in three days.

The shutdown was supposed to be for seven days but after being closed for more than six weeks I called to ask when I could expect the inspector to return to approve the changes. I was told that it may be two more months before and I would have to attend a hearing with the board for them to decide if I could open. I knew I could not continue to be closed for two more months without facing financial bankruptcy.

I prayed and once again placed the burden on the Lord to help me overcome this mountain. The barber board was the final authority for issuing licenses for schools or barbers, but they were appointed by the governor, so I decided to contact the governor's office. I drove three and a half hours to Jackson, Mississippi to the governor's office where I received information on how to email a complaint to the governor. Once I emailed the complaint that evening, I received a phone call from the Attorney General's office. I exposed everything without leaving out any details about my situation and asked why I wasn't being allowed to open. The person from the Attorney General's office told me to wait by my phone and expect a phone call.

The next morning, I went to the building and walked the entire perimeter praying to God. It was a man from the barber board on the phone, and he told me he was going to try to get an inspector to my building that day. When I hung up the phone, in less than five minutes a building inspector was at the door. He went through the checklist of requirements, and everything had been done. I was given approval for the relocation and the ability to reopen the school. If I would have kept quiet, the issue would not have been resolved and I would have continued to live in fear.

Yes, the barber board had power but the One with all power in His hands gave me the vision, so I used the greatest weapon to overcome fear and doubt in any situation. PRAYER.

I don't know what is ahead for the school, but I know God is in control and He will provide.

"Do not be anxious about anything, but in every situation, by prayer and petition, with thanksgiving, present your requests to God. And the peace of God, which transcends all understanding, will guard your hearts and your minds in Christ Jesus." ~ Philippians 4:6-7

I firmly believe that everything that has happened in my life has prepared me for the mission God has for me. I am stronger in my faith and belief in God because of all the tests that God brought me through. No one and nothing can make me doubt Him because I have experienced His miracles, mercies and grace for myself.

Every time the devil tried to destroy the college, God provided me with a better building and greater opportunities. When I look back on how I was struggling to stay in those places it was as if I was trying to hold onto an old raggedy car when God was offering me a Porsche. When I finally let go and submitted to whatever God's will was for me, I had a smooth transition in the comfort of God's peace. All of the past history provides confirmation that the vision was from God and greater will continue in his name.

Chapter Twenty-Nine

By experience I have learned dark times come, but I have to be confident that the Lord is in control. In the past whenever I took my eyes off God and tried to handle my problems on my own it would always make a bad situation worse. Satan doesn't fight fair. He has no boundaries. He delivers low blows by attacking you through those closest to you: your family, friends, church members and even strangers are not excluded as part of his weaponry. Until you recognize who he is and learn to discern the onset of his attack you will always find yourself against the ropes in a boxing match with the devil. You can't win the battle by yourself. Wisdom has taught me not to fight but to pray. Through prayer I will have the victory because my strength comes from God. God has never lost a battle. According to Hebrews 11:1, "Now faith is the substance of things hoped for, the evidence of things not seen." The principles of the promises to Believers are given freely. There is a lot that we are able to obtain by that verse alone.

The promises are available to all who believe in God. The difference between having a vision come to fruition and it never materializing is in utilizing the principles of faith and in what you put your faith and/or trust in. You must not only believe but you must put your belief in action by faith. You can believe and hope for something, but you have to put it into action. With no action, all you have is a dream.

Faith is the substance for which hope is based. By definition a substance is a particular kind of matter with uniform properties. The real physical matter of which a person or thing consists of and which has a tangible, solid presence. I make a conscious choice to believe in the Creator not a creation.

In other words, faith is something that has matter. If you are a Christian, your faith is based on the fact that God is because he exists all matter has its being through and by Him. Once I professed Jesus Christ to be my Savior, I became an heir to the promises of God. Understanding that concept opened doors for me that I had closed through my doubt and unbelief. When I changed my thoughts, I was able to clear my mind of and worry, gloom and doom.

I thank God for the spiritual leaders that he placed in my life. Each appeared in a special season when they were needed most.

I thank him for Pastor John Hoover who was there through my childhood years. He started me on my quest for the knowledge of God and gave me the good strong advice to always search the scriptures for myself.

I was blessed by God to be under the spiritual leadership of Pastor Joseph and Becky Drake who taught me how to pray according to the scriptures. They introduced me to the 5-fold ministry and literally gave me the keys to walking in the belief of God's healing power.

I thank God for my season with Bishop David Ritchie and Pastor Margaret who taught me the importance of prayer and being a doer and not just a hearer of the Lord's word and most importantly to move on your faith.

Lastly, I thank my current spiritual leader, Bishop Torien and Alicia Preston for words of encouragement and the ability to recognize that we are all human and we make mistakes, but God's grace is sufficient to help us recover and his willingness to teach others how to use the power of faith. Under these leaders, I learned to trust and have faith in God. It has not been easy. I failed the test many times. I stayed on that merry-go-round of making bad decisions to fill voids in my life. Until I recognized what the voids were and asked God to fill the emptiness, I continued repeating the same test. I placed my desire to have a relationship with a man ahead of being obedient to God and patiently waiting for him to send me the person I needed. When I backed off and searched to have more knowledge of Him, He provided me with my soulmate for 19 years, Matthew Mims.

I thank God for the trials and tribulations because I learned how to react in accordance with the will of God. To use prayer when I feel the darkness come over me. I have learned to recognize when Satan was setting a trap for me and to not cut myself off from God's light. We are told in James 1:22, "But be doers of the word, and not hearers only, deceiving yourselves." (NIV)

I learned to put my faith in action by submitting to the understanding that God was in control of any situation. Sometimes it took me a few moments to recognize I was going in the wrong direction but now I know how to reposition myself to be in God's grace and walk in His eternal light.

Satan's greatest accomplishment would be to come between you and God. Once separation occurs, he can have a field day with your mind. His agenda is to make you doubt yourself and your God-given purpose for your life. Once he knows you are insecure in yourself, his next move is to find a way to separate you from other believers. It makes you easy prey for the devil to destroy your dreams. The true saints of God will encourage each other not to give up the fight and to have faith that there is VICTORY in God no matter the situation. When dark times come now instead of allowing myself to dwell on things as I see them with my natural eyes, I must envision them through spiritual eyes of faith as though it has already materialized for my good. Because of the trials and tribulations in my past and my testimony of God always showing up on time my faith in Him has increased. I can truly say with confidence that I can do all things through Christ who strengthens me. Philippians 4:16. Just like my school logo I place my life in God's hands; I have been through the shadow of death and because my faith in God has strengthened, I know that the shadow is just a temporary separation from light. The shadow only stays as long as you allow yourself to be blocked from the light. The shadow of death doesn't have the ability to hurt me, but my fear of it can wreak havoc on my mind and body. The doctors can tell me that I am going to die tomorrow. I can choose to believe it and worry myself until I experience a heart attack which would be the cause of my death, or I can choose life and say my life is in God's hands and bypass the emotional distress. Faith in God allows me to be free from fear of the shadows of death because when death comes, I have the promise of eternal life. I have no fear of the shadows of this life because I know it's only a shadow and that's my clue to reposition myself in God's light.

Printed in Great Britain
by Amazon